POSITIV

AFFIRMATIONS

#IAM

EMPOWER & ELEVATE EACH DAY

LISTEN UPLIFT VENT
C.I.C

ABOUT US

#IAM Sara Maynard, the founder of
Listen Uplift Vent CIC.

LUV was created to provide women and
young girls with a platform to develop,
grow and be the best the version of
themselves.
At LUV we believe affirmations are an
important part of daily life.
By reciting positive affirmations on a
daily basis, you can make REAL changes
to your life.

It all starts with your mindset.

Introduction

♥♥

This little book is filled with positive
affirmations.

Every thought you think and every word
you speak is an affirmation. So why not
choose to use only positive affirmations
to Empower and Elevate your life?

#IAM Positive Affirmation book is here
to help you uplift your daily life. Each
day when you arise, recite out loud
the verses from this book. If necessary,
repeat until
you feel it clinging to your soul.

#IAM

Beautiful just as I am

We should never allow anybody else's thoughts or feelings make us question our beauty

#IAM

Grateful for every experience in each moment of my life

We must appreciate all we experience in life; the good and the bad, as they all have purpose

#IAM

Allowed
to fail

We should stop looking at failure
as a negative and start to look at it
as a lesson

#IAM

ENOUGH

PERIOD;
Nothing more needs to be said!!

#IAM

Never alone

Even though we may feel as though we are alone, there is always someone there who is willing to Listen to you, Uplift you and allow you to Vent

LISTEN UPLIFT VEN
C.I.C

Empower :: Educate :: Elevate through Self-LUV

#IAM

More than what you see

Others may judge you based on what they see on the exterior. Never forget you are more than what you look like or wear. Your heart and how you treat yourself and others is what is important

#IAM

Focusing on the positivity for a better me

Although it may not be easy sometimes, try to focus on the positive even in negative situations.
Remain focused!!

#IAM

Mentally & emotionally equipped to start enjoy a loving prosperous life

By adjusting your thoughts and changing your mindset, you will be able to use the right tools to enjoy life – That is your birth right!!

#IAM

Loved

You may not feel it sometimes,
but you most definately are loved.
The best type of love is Self-LUV

#IAM

Proud of who I am becoming

Each day is a new day to grow. Be proud you are taking action on wanting to create a better mindset. It all starts with YOU

#IAM

Focused, persistent and will never quit

You are capable of doing anything you put your mind to!! Even on days where you may feel low, take a day off for Self-LUV. You got this!!

#IAM

Brave

You may not feel it or believe it at times but you are! Getting up and facing each day is an accomplishment within itself

#IAM

In charge

You are in control of your life, the decisions / choices you make. Make them count!! Become the best version of YOU

#IAM

ME

And that is what makes you unique!! There will never be another YOU, so own it and love yourself for who you are!!

#IAM

Journal

This next section of the book is dedicated to you speaking your truth unapologetically. Please don't forget that we are humans, who have feelings and emotions that are there to be felt. However, do not allow these to consume you for too long as this will be detrimental to your mental well-being. Take note of them, identify any triggers, understand how it made you think, the feelings you felt but focus on how you can change this response. Remember that sometimes it is ok, to not be ok!

Today I am feeling;

This was triggered by:

This made me feel:

What do you need to change to prevent these thoughts, feelings & reactions next time?

What did you do in reaction:

Today I am feeling;

This was triggered by:

This made me feel:

What do you need to change to prevent these thoughts, feelings & reactions next time?

What did you do in reaction:

Today I am feeling;

This was triggered by:

This made me feel:

What do you need to change to prevent these thoughts, feelings & reactions next time?

What did you do in reaction:

Today I am feeling;

This was triggered by:

This made me feel:

What do you need to change to prevent these thoughts, feelings & reactions next time?

What did you do in
reaction:

Today I am feeling;

This was triggered by:

This made me feel:

What do you need to change to prevent these thoughts, feelings & reactions next time?

What did you do in
reaction:

Today I am feeling;

This was triggered by:

This made me feel:

What do you need to change to prevent these thoughts, feelings & reactions next time?

What did you do in reaction:

Today I am feeling;

This was triggered by:

This made me feel:

What do you need to change to prevent these thoughts, feelings & reactions next time?

What did you do in reaction:

Today I am feeling;

This was triggered by:

This made me feel:

What do you need to change to prevent these thoughts, feelings & reactions next time?

What did you do in reaction:

Today I am feeling;

This was triggered by:

This made me feel:

What do you need to change to prevent these thoughts, feelings & reactions next time?

What did you do in reaction:

Today I am feeling;

This was triggered by:

This made me feel:

What do you need to change to prevent these thoughts, feelings & reactions next time?

What did you do in reaction:

#IAM

Becoming the best version of ME

Author: Sara Maynard

Editor: Adella Fletcher

LISTEN UPLIFT VENT
C.I.C

Empower ❤ Educate ❤ Elevate through Self-LUV

Printed in Great Britain
by Amazon